AF382454

MAINBEAST
PUBLISHING

If I could know the absolute truth to one question,
I would ask:

What is the essence of human existence, the profound
purpose that lies woven within the tapestry of our lives?

IF YOU COULD *KNOW* THE ABSOLUTE TRUTH TO *ONE* QUESTION.

WHAT WOULD YOU ASK?

Amidst the vastness of the cosmos, we are tiny specks, yet we hold the capacity to create, to love, to experience the depths of emotion. What is the significance of our existence in this grand scheme?

The pursuit of happiness often leads us astray, for it's not a destination but a journey, a continuous process of learning, growth, and connection. What is the true meaning of fulfillment, the state where we feel fully alive and engaged in the world?

We are all born into a world of inherent paradoxes: joy and sorrow, love and loss, light and darkness. How can we navigate these complexities, finding meaning and resilience amidst the swings of human experience?

The human mind is a vast universe, capable of both
profound insights and self-destructive tendencies.
How can we harness the power of our thoughts for
positive change, transforming our inner landscape?

Relationships are the cornerstone of our existence,
shaping our perceptions of self and the world. What
is the essence of true connection, the bond that
transcends superficiality and resonates deeply?

Death is an inevitable part of life, a stark reminder of our finite existence. How can we approach this inevitability with wisdom and acceptance, finding solace in the knowledge of our legacy?

We are not mere bystanders in the grand narrative of life;
we are active participants, responsible for shaping our
own destinies and the world around us. What is the ethical
framework that guides our actions, ensuring a harmonious
coexistence with others and the environment?

Creativity is the language of the soul, a means of expressing our deepest emotions, thoughts, and experiences. What is the role of art, music, and literature in illuminating the human condition and fostering empathy?

Faith, spirituality, and the search for meaning
transcend the boundaries of conventional religion.
What is the nature of the divine, the force that
connects us to something greater than ourselves?

We are constantly evolving, adapting to the
changing tides of life. What is the power of resilience,
the ability to rise from setbacks and embrace the
transformative potential of change?

Our planet is a fragile oasis in the vast expanse of the universe, a precious life-giving force that we must cherish and protect. What is our responsibility to environmental stewardship, ensuring the well-being of future generations?

Technology is a double-edged sword, wielding the potential to both connect and divide, liberate and enslave. What is the ethical framework for technological advancement, ensuring that it serves humanity's best interests?

Education is not merely about acquiring knowledge; it's about cultivating critical thinking, empathy, and the ability to navigate the complexities of the modern world. What is the role of education in shaping a more just and equitable society?

The arts are not mere entertainment; they are windows into the human spirit, offering insights into our deepest emotions, fears, and aspirations. What is the importance of the arts in fostering cultural understanding and personal growth?

We are all interconnected, bound by a shared humanity that transcends race, religion, and nationality. What is the power of compassion, the ability to see ourselves in others and treat them with dignity and respect?

Forgiveness is not about condoning wrongdoings;
it's about releasing ourselves from the shackles of
resentment and finding peace within. What is the
transformative power of forgiveness, enabling us to
move forward with grace and understanding?

Our actions have ripple effects that extend far beyond our immediate circles. What is the importance of ethical decision-making, considering the consequences of our choices on ourselves, others, and the environment?

We are not alone in this vast universe; there may be other forms of life out there, sharing our curiosity and yearning for connection. What is the possibility of extraterrestrial life, and what would it mean for our understanding of our place in the cosmos?

Time is a precious commodity, finite and irreplaceable. What is the wisdom of living in the present moment, appreciating the fleeting nature of life and finding joy in the here and now?

Our legacy is not determined by material possessions but by the impact we have on others, the actions we take, and the values we embody. What is the essence of a meaningful life, one that leaves a lasting imprint on the world?

We are all storytellers, weaving our narratives into the fabric of human experience. What is the power of storytelling, the ability to connect with others on a profound level through shared experiences and emotions?

Dreams are not mere figments of our imagination; they hold a symbolic significance, reflecting our deepest desires, fears, and aspirations. What is the role of dreams in guiding our conscious lives and unlocking our potential?

Intuition is a subtle yet powerful force, a guiding
voice that whispers within our hearts. What is
the wisdom of listening to our intuition, allowing
it to steer us towards our authentic path?

Solitude is not a state of loneliness but a
sanctuary for introspection and personal growth.
What is the importance of finding balance
between connection and solitude, nurturing our
inner world alongside our relationships?

Gratitude is the antidote to discontent, shifting our focus from what we lack to the blessings we already possess. What is the power of cultivating gratitude, allowing us to appreciate the richness of our lives?

Hope is the beacon that guides us through darkness, illuminating the path towards a brighter future. What is the resilience of hope, the unwavering belief in the possibility of good even amidst adversity?

Love is the ultimate force that binds us together, transcending boundaries and connecting us to something greater than ourselves. What is the true nature of love, the essence that nurtures our souls and transforms the world?

Compassion is the foundation of a just and compassionate society, extending empathy and understanding to all beings. What is the power of compassion to heal wounds, bridge divides, and create a more harmonious world?

Forgiveness is not about forgetting but about
releasing the burden of anger and resentment,
allowing ourselves to heal and move forward.
What is the transformative power of forgiveness,
fostering reconciliation and peace of mind?

Courage is not the absence of fear but the willingness to act despite it. What is the power of courage to overcome obstacles, pursue our dreams, and make a difference in the world?

Humility is not about self-deprecation but about recognizing our limitations and appreciating the wisdom of others. What is the transformative power of humility to foster connection, growth, and a deeper understanding of ourselves?

Integrity is the cornerstone of a fulfilling life, acting with honesty, authenticity, and moral compass. What is the importance of integrity to building trust, maintaining meaningful relationships, and living a life of purpose?

Non-violence is not about submission but about the
power of peaceful resistance, challenging injustice
and promoting compassion. What is the role of non-
violence in creating a more just and equitable world?

Mindfulness is the practice of living in the
present moment, observing our thoughts
and emotions without judgment. What is the
power of mindfulness to reduce stress,
improve focus, and cultivate inner peace?

Self-acceptance is the foundation of self-love, embracing our imperfections and celebrating our unique individuality. What is the importance of self-acceptance to fostering self-confidence, resilience, and a sense of wholeness?

Service is not about selflessness but about finding joy in giving back and making a positive impact on the world. What is the power of service to connect us to a sense of purpose and belonging?

Sustainable living is not just an environmental imperative but a moral obligation to future generations. What are the challenges and opportunities of living in harmony with nature, ensuring the well-being of our planet for generations to come?

Universalism is the recognition of shared humanity,
embracing our diversity while recognizing our
common values and aspirations. What is the power
of universalism to foster empathy, understanding,
and a more just and equitable world?

Transcendental experiences are moments of profound connection to something greater than ourselves, suggesting the existence of a deeper reality beyond the physical world. What are the implications of these experiences for our understanding of consciousness, the nature of reality, and our place in the universe?

Mysticism is the exploration of the inner realms of consciousness, seeking to transcend the limitations of the physical world and connect with the divine. What are the insights and challenges of mystical experiences, and what role do they play in the human quest for meaning?

Spirituality is not confined to organized religion but encompasses a broader search for meaning and connection to something greater than ourselves. What is the essence of spirituality, and how can we cultivate it in our own lives?

Death is not an ending but a transition, a passage into an unknown realm. What are the philosophical and spiritual implications of death, and how can we approach it with wisdom and acceptance?

Afterlife beliefs vary across cultures and
traditions, suggesting the enduring human desire
to understand the nature of death and what lies
beyond. What are the implications of afterlife
beliefs for our understanding of life,death, and
the meaning of existence?

Consciousness is a mystery that has baffled
philosophers and scientists for centuries.
What is the nature of consciousness, and
how does it arise from a physical brain?

Free will is the ability to make choices independently of external influences. What is the role of free will in shaping our lives and determining our destinies?

Karma and reincarnation are concepts that suggest a cyclical nature of existence, with our actions and choices having consequences in future lives. What are the implications of these beliefs for our understanding of morality,responsibility, and personal growth?

Simulation theory proposes that we might be living in a computer simulation, questioning our perception of reality and the nature of consciousness. What are the implications of simulation theory for our understanding of our place in the cosmos?

The multiverse hypothesis suggests that
there might be multiple universes, each with
its own unique laws of physics and existence.
What are the implications of the multiverse
hypothesis for our understanding of the
universe and our place within it?

The ultimate question of all human existence:
What is the meaning of life?

Is it a journey of self-discovery, a quest for purpose, or
a divine plan? What is the essence of a meaningful
life that leaves a lasting impact on the world?